Lustige Madrigalien und Canzonetten

Recent Researches in Music

A-R Editions publishes seven series of critical editions, spanning the history of Western music, American music, and oral traditions.

Recent Researches in the Music of the Middle Ages and Early Renaissance
  Charles M. Atkinson, general editor

Recent Researches in the Music of the Renaissance
  James Haar, general editor

Recent Researches in the Music of the Baroque Era
  Christoph Wolff, general editor

Recent Researches in the Music of the Classical Era
  Eugene K. Wolf, general editor

Recent Researches in the Music of the Nineteenth and Early Twentieth Centuries
  Rufus Hallmark, general editor

Recent Researches in American Music
  John M. Graziano, general editor

Recent Researches in the Oral Traditions of Music
  Philip V. Bohlman, general editor

Each edition in *Recent Researches* is devoted to works by a single composer or to a single genre. The content is chosen for its high quality and historical importance, and each edition includes a substantial introduction and critical report. The music is engraved according to the highest standards of production using the proprietary software MusE, owned by Music│Notes.™

For information on establishing a standing order to any of our series, or for editorial guidelines on submitting proposals, please contact:

A-R Editions, Inc.
801 Deming Way
Madison, Wisconsin 53717

800 736-0070 (U.S. book orders)
608 836-9000 (phone)
608 831-8200 (fax)
http://www.areditions.com

Acknowledgments

The present edition was instigated and prepared by Bernd Baselt. Prior to his untimely death in 1993, Prof. Baselt had submitted his manuscript of the score together with a draft of his introduction and critical report. A-R Editions asked me to assist them in completing the project. I carefully proofread the edition against the original source, making a number of minor adjustments, and provided a new introduction that is mostly based on my own research; only for the sections "The Music" and "The Texts and Their Authors" have I made use of Prof. Baselt's material. In general, I have tried to follow Prof. Baselt's intentions as closely as possible. Finally, I wish to express my gratitude to Ms. Elfriede Baselt, who kindly placed her late husband's notes at my disposal.

Peter Wollny

Contents

Sebastian Knüpfer

Lustige Madrigalien und Canzonetten

Edited by Bernd Baselt

Introduction by Peter Wollny

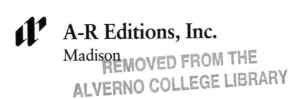

A-R Editions, Inc.

Madison

Performance parts are available from the publisher.

A-R Editions, Inc., Madison, Wisconsin 53717
© 1999 by A-R Editions, Inc.

A-R Editions is pleased to support scholars and performers in their use of *Recent Researches* material for study or performance. Subscribers to any of the *Recent Researches* series, as well as patrons of subscribing institutions, are invited to apply for information about our "Copyright Sharing Policy."

Printed in the United States of America

ISBN 0-89579-431-4
ISSN 0484-0828

⊖ The paper used in this publication meets the minimum requirements of the American National Standard for Information Sciences—Permanence of Paper for Printed Library Materials, ANSI Z39.48-1984.

Introduction

In the fall of 1663, the biennially released Leipzig trading fair catalogs announcing newly printed books listed the following anthology with secular compositions by the Thomaskantor and *Director musices:* "Sebastian Knüpfers lustige Madrigalien und Canzonetten. 4. [i.e., quarto] Leipzig in Verlag Christian Kirchners."[1] Twenty-three years later the same periodical announced a second edition of Knüpfer's collection, this time printed by "Friedrich Lankischens Erben." A more precise bibliographic reference was given by Johann Gottfried Walther, who apparently had access to a copy of the first edition and from the preface of the anthology gleaned biographical data for his *Musicalisches Lexicon* of 1732.[2] Subsequent lexicographers had to rely on the information provided by Walther, as soon every copy of the *Lustige Madrigalien* appeared to be lost.

Thus Knüpfer's madrigals were not available when Arnold Schering published his *Denkmäler* volume *Sebastian Knüpfer, Johann Schelle, Johann Kuhnau: Ausgewählte Kirchenkantaten* (1918/19)[3] and the second part of his *Musikgeschichte Leipzigs* (1926), treating the late seventeenth and early eighteenth centuries.[4] To be sure, around 1902 a single part (*Prima Vox*) of the *Lustige Madrigalien* had been traced in a church library at Sorau,[5] but the small yet significant music collection containing it was destroyed only a short while after the scholarly world had become aware of it.[6]

It thus came as a complete surprise when, in 1932, in connection with Hans Joachim Moser's research for his book on the German baroque lied a complete copy of Knüpfer's madrigal collection surfaced at the Bibliothek der Allgemeinen Musikgesellschaft in Zurich; since the discovery happened only after Moser had nearly completed his book, the collection's historical and musical significance are discussed only briefly, while four of its numbers are published in the accompanying anthology.[7] Yet the full musical and historical significance of the *Lustige Madrigalien* can only be understood from a complete edition of the entire group of twenty pieces. These form a welcome addition to our knowledge of the typical repertory of an academic collegium musicum in the mid seventeenth century.

The Composer

Sebastian Knüpfer's reputation as a composer is mainly based on his sacred music. This is reflected in his obituary, published shortly after his death on 10 October 1676, which points out the delightfulness and artistry found in his settings of psalms and other biblical texts.[8] There are only few contemporary documents on Knüpfer's biography surviving, and these shed light mostly on his activities as Thomaskantor, a position he held from 1657 until his death. Little is known about the earlier period of his life, during which he gradually built up his reputation, which eventually led to his being offered one of the most prestigious musical posts in middle Germany.

The main stages of Knüpfer's youth and education are briefly described in the above-mentioned obituary. According to this document, he was born on 6 September 1633, in Asch (now Aš, situated in the Czech Republic), then a small town in the Erzgebirge region of southern Saxony, located about half-way between Dresden and Nuremberg. His father was the local organist and cantor Johannes Knüpfer, from whom Sebastian received his first education and musical training. By the time he reached the age of ten, his masterful playing of the organ was attracting public attention. In 1646, Knüpfer entered the famous Gymnasium Poeticum at Regensburg, where he was a student for the following eight years. While no details of Knüpfer's education in Regensburg are available, it is most likely that he met local musicians such as the organists and composers Augustin and Hieronymus Kradenthaler.

In 1654, a scholarship awarded to him by the city council of Regensburg enabled Knüpfer to move to Leipzig in order to further his education at the university. Probably due to contacts established for him by his Regensburg patrons, he was invited to stay in the house of Johann Philippi, professor of law at the University of Leipzig and a member of the city council. Knüpfer became the teacher of Philippi's son Christian, the dedicatee of the *Lustige Madrigalien*. It is puzzling, however, that Knüpfer's name does not appear in the university's matriculation lists. But even if he did not officially enroll as a student, he apparently was able to establish close contact with academic life at Leipzig and was particularly active within the city's musical circles. He most certainly became a member of the collegium musicum, which was directed by Johann Rosenmüller until he had to leave the town in 1655 and thereafter by Adam Krieger. There is some indication that at the time the collegium musicum was involved in the music performances at Leipzig's two main churches, St. Thomas and St. Nicolai, directed by the Thomaskantor Tobias Michael. In 1657, Knüpfer succeeded Michael in his office; the protocol documenting his application state that he had performed as a bass singer in the Leipzig churches.

Soon after his installation as Thomaskantor, Knüpfer married Maria Sabina Hagen, the daughter of a Leipzig merchant. The couple had five children; their oldest son, Johann Magnus, followed in the footsteps of his father and became a musician.[9]

As Thomaskantor, Knüpfer's main compositional activities consisted of providing sacred works for the church service. Today, about two hundred sacred vocal compositions can be documented, about a third of them surviving in musical sources.[10] Their chronology has not been tackled so far, and therefore any statements about Knüpfer's stylistic development can only be preliminary. Some clues are given by a number of sources from the collection of the former Fürstenschule at Grimma (now kept at the Sächsische Landesbibliothek in Dresden).[11] It is generally assumed that the main scribe and former owner of this collection, the Grimma cantor Samuel Jacobi (1652–1721), had access to musical repertoires from Leipzig, most likely even to original manuscripts written by Knüpfer and his successors Johann Schelle and Johann Kuhnau. In his copies of four large-scale sacred concertos by Knüpfer, Jacobi noted their dates of composition ("1669 mens Mart.," "[16]70," "1672. mens. Dec.," and "Mens Maji 1676"). Could this mean that the fully scored pieces mostly represent late works, while the smaller concertos tend to stem from the early phase of Knüpfer's tenure as cantor?

A hitherto unnoticed clue for the dating of Knüpfer's earlier sacred works is given in his preface to the *Lustige Madrigalien:* "But in the near future the first part of my sacred concertos for 1, 2, 3, 4, 5, and 6 voices and various instruments (some of which can be omitted if desired) is to follow." As far as is known, this edition never materialized, but most of the works intended for the collection must already have been composed when the announcement was published. It is difficult to ascertain whether any of these pieces circulated in manuscript after the plan to publish them was aborted, and it is even more difficult to determine whether any of Knüpfer's surviving works belong to this group. The title he chose for the intended collection suggests that in certain details he followed his predecessor Tobias Michael's *Musicalischer Seelen-Lust ander Theil* (1637), which contained concertos "In mancherley Art mit 1–6 und mehr Stimmen, abgewechselten Instrumenten, Symphonien und Capellen" ("in various manners, for 1–6 and more voices, varying instruments, symphonies, and capellas"). Other models may have been the two parts of Rosenmüller's *Kernsprüche* (1648 and 1652/53) and the late works of Heinrich Schütz.

Knüpfer's mentioning, in the preface of his *Lustige Madrigalien,* of his "particularly good friend" David Elias Heidenreich provides the context for another series of his sacred music. The Halle court poet and former Leipzig student Heidenreich is the author of an annual cycle of cantata texts that was published in 1665 as *Geistliche Oden auf die fürnehmsten Feste und alle Sonntage des gantzen Jahres.* From Heidenreich's preface to this collection we learn that the first composer to set these texts to music was the Halle kapellmeister David Pohle;[12] judging from the close contacts between Knüpfer and Heidenreich, however, it is likely that Knüpfer, too, came to know and set Heidenreich's innovative poetry soon after it appeared in print. Although only ten cantatas set by Knüpfer on texts from the *Geistliche Oden* survive,[13] it is more than feasible that he composed music for the entire collection of 66 poems.

Apart from his duties as Thomaskantor, Knüpfer appears to have continued to work with the academic collegium musicum, although it remains unclear whether he ever functioned as its director. His constant involvement with literary and musical student circles is documented (1) by the dedicatory sonnet to *Lustige Madrigalien,* addressed to him by the collegium musicum; (2) by his funeral ode and canon commemorating the death of the Leipzig organist Gerhard Preisensin (1672), published with the note "performed by the collegium musicum"; and (3) by a collection of poetry written by the Leipzig student Martin Kempe and published in 1665 as *Poetische Lust-Gedanken;* each of the two parts of this collection contains a poem dedicated to "the famous musician" Knüpfer.[14]

In his preface to *Lustige Madrigalien,* Knüpfer mentions that in addition to the pieces selected for the print he has composed "a considerable number of similar pieces, which will also see the light of day should the present selection meet with a favorable reception." Yet no further pieces from his manuscript collection of secular pieces appear ever to have been printed and there are only a few references to this repertory in contemporary inventories, suggesting that they did not circulate widely. The famous Leipzig inventory of 1712, which contains the musical estate of Knüpfer's successor Johann Schelle, in addition to a "Sonata super Guten Abend Garten Mann," lists three secular pieces attributed to Knüpfer that are not included in *Lustige Madrigalien:* "Drey schöne Dinge sind," "Es kömpt ein neuer Schleifer an," and "Höret wunderschöne Sachen."[15] Moreover, the inventory of the Lüneburg Michaelisschule lists a two-part secular composition by Knüpfer entitled "Leipziger Kehr-Michels Erster und anderer Theil (F♭)."[16] While none of these pieces have survived, another secular composition that has hitherto escaped notice is found in the Düben collection.[17] This piece is transmitted in a set of performing parts copied by an unknown scribe not appearing elsewhere in the Düben collection; the title page of its continuo part bears the following inscription: *Laßt uns den fürnen Wein:* | *â 6.* | *2 Violin* | *Canto.* | *Alto.* | *Tenore* | *Basso.* | *di.* | *S. K.* The musical style of this work as well as its text (a drinking song similar to no. 1 of the present collection) suggest that it was composed around the same time and probably belonged to the group of pieces that Knüpfer referred to in his preface. A different type of secular composition is represented by the occasional madrigal "Glück zu! Dieweil der milde Sachse," written for a celebration of the Leipzig town council and published in 1658.[18]

An important aspect of Knüpfer's musical personality was his intense interest in ancient and medieval music theory. As his obituary puts it, he was "a friend of classical culture" and studied the Greek writings on music from a volume that had just been edited by Marcus Meibom.[19] He is also said to have copied musical treatises by Guido of Arezzo, Boethius, and Berno of Reichenau, which he found at the Bibliotheca Paulina (the Leipzig university library); the exemplars he copied from may be identical with the manuscripts *Cod. 1493, Cod. 1305,* and *Cod. 1492* still kept as precious holdings at the manuscript department of the present Universitätsbibliothek.[20] The frequently cited claim that Knüpfer prepared printed editions of these treatises, however, is probably based on an erroneous translation of the Latin term "excussit" used in the obituary in connection with Knüpfer's studying ancient treatises on music theory;[21] as becomes clear from the context, "excussere" here is not used in the sense of "to publish" but rather in the Ovidian meaning of "to examine, to investigate, or to scrutinize."[22] These philological interests were part of Knüpfer's broad humanistic horizon, which also induced him to study philosophy with the Leipzig professor Johann Adam Scherzer even after he had been appointed Thomaskantor.

In keeping with his historical and theoretical interests, Knüpfer's compositional style is firmly rooted in the polyphonic tradition, praised by Schütz as the true fundament of composition. His music, however, does not reveal any archaic tendencies but due to an imaginative and at times extremely expressive use of harmony is very much at the height of its time. Knüpfer's thorough contrapuntal treatment of the musical texture—alluded to in a number of contemporary documents by a pun on his name ("knüpfen" meaning "entwining" or "knotting together")—is mainly found in his sacred works, but can also be traced in his secular compositions, where it is mostly used in a much lighter fashion.

Both the high esteem in which he was generally held and the wide distribution of his music—evident in the fact that his works are present in numerous contemporary inventories[23]—mark Knüpfer as a central figure in German music history of the seventeenth century. This outstanding position was already firmly established by the time he died from a malign fever in October 1676, having only reached the age of 43. In light of his overall achievement the closing remarks of the obituary, according to which Knüpfer was a musician that "Leipzig neither saw before nor . . . shall ever see again," are by no means to be dismissed as a poetic exaggeration.

The Music

The twenty pieces collected in *Lustige Madrigalien* not only document an important facet of Knüpfer's early period, but together with the collections by Adam Krieger (1657, 1667), Johann Theile (1667), and Johann Caspar Horn (1674, 1678) represent a most significant contribution to the German lied tradition.[24] As Knüpfer writes in his preface, the pieces assembled in *Lustige Madrigalien* had "been composed a long time ago," in fact the entire opus had been ready for print for several years. It is therefore feasible that most, if not all of these works, stem from the early years of his Leipzig period, that is, from about 1654–57. This may also be the reason why much of the preface consists of a justification for publishing music that wasn't new anymore and that did not fit in well with the duties and dignity of Knüpfer's office as Thomaskantor. (A complete transcription and translation of the preface is given below in the appendix.)

The two genres are arranged in such a way that the through-composed a capella continuo madrigals alternate with the strophically organized canzonettas, only the latter are to be performed with instrumentally enriched accompaniment. The single exception to this rule is the first madrigal, which could be labelled a concertato madrigal.[25] Its two violin parts are, however, marked *si placet* and *se piace* respectively. Of those numbers designated as madrigals, which with few exceptions follow a two-part formal layout, sometimes with coda, only six (nos. 1, 3, 5, 7, 9, and 11) represent genuine madrigals according to Werner Braun's definition of the genre, that is, they contain at least four vocal parts and continuo or further optional instrumental accompaniment.[26] The four madrigals for fewer voices (nos. 13, 15, and 17 for three voices, and no. 19 for two voices) display the same formal layout and quite similar compositional techiques. All the madrigals exhibit the expected flexibility of musical features with varying density of texture, an expressive use of harmony and a preference for "affective, rather than descriptive" melodic design.[27] Only the final madrigal (no. 19) might rather be seen as Knüpfer's contribution to the genre of the chamber duet.

The pieces labelled canzonettas are based on strophic texts or, as Knüpfer calls them, odes. Despite the formal limitations of their textual structure, the composer was able to create great variety both between the different pieces and within the individual works themselves. Most of the pieces can be characterized as concertato canzonettas with two voices, predominantly syllabic text declamation and at least two instrumental ritornellos played by two violins.[28] Knüpfer varies this scheme by occasionally employing one or three voices and by experimenting with different instrumental combinations.

The canzonettas display basically two different formal schemes, a two-part form (found in nos. 2, 4, 12, 14, 18, and 20) and a three-part form (found in nos. 6 and 16). These two schemes may be laid out as follows:

1. Two-part form. Sonata (usually in duple meter) followed by the first vocal section (musically related to the preceding sonata), then a ritornello (often in triple meter) followed by a second vocal section (musically related to the preceding ritornello).

2. Three-part form. Sonata (in duple meter) followed by the first vocal section (musically related to the preceding sonata), then a ritornello (in triple meter) followed by a second vocal section (musically related to the preceding ritornello) with a third vocal section (in duple meter).

The canzonettas nos. 8 and 10 display an even more complex structure. No. 10 is an entirely through-composed setting with instrumental sonatas preceding each stanza of the text; the highly sophisticated musical correspondences between the different sections appear to have been inspired by Schütz's canzonetta "Tugend ist der beste Freund" (SWV 442) on a poem by Martin Opitz.[29] No. 8, on the other hand, provides two different musical settings for one stanza each, and assigns stanzas 1, 3, and 6 to the first and stanzas 2, 4, and 5 to the second setting; this results in the formal structure of A–B–A–B–B–A.

The Texts and Their Authors

Knüpfer points out that as many as eleven of the poems he set to music for the *Lustige Madrigalien* (the madrigals nos. 1, 5, 11, 15, and the canzonettas nos. 2, 4, 8, 12, 14, 18, 20) were written by David Elias Heidenreich.[30] Born in Leipzig in 1638, Heidenreich studied theology and literature at the local university and during that time published his first poetic essays as well as his translations of dramas by Joost van Vondel, Thomas Corneille, and Des Marets. After completing his studies at Leipzig, Heidenreich held various administrative positions at the courts of Halle (until 1680) and Weißenfels (until his death in 1688). He also was a member of the "Fruchtbringende Gesellschaft," a German literary society. Apart from writing the above-mentioned cycle of cantata texts (Halle, 1665), Heidenreich was the librettist for numerous operas performed at Halle and Weißenfels between 1667 and 1687.

The author of two further pieces (nos. 6 and 16) is identified by Knüpfer as Johann Georg Schoch. Schoch was born in Leipzig in 1634; he studied law in his home town and subsequently held administrative positions at Naumburg, Westerburg, Cölln/Spree, and Braunschweig; he died around 1690.[31] The two poems set by Knüpfer were published in a collection of Schoch's poetry that appeared in Leipzig in 1660.[32] The authors of the remaining seven pieces (nos. 3, 7, 9, 10, 13, 17, and 19) have not yet been identified. It would probably be worthwhile to search for them in poetry collections published around 1650–1660 in Leipzig or nearby places.

Appendix

Preface to *Lustige Madrigalien und Canzonetten*

An den Leser.
Es werden sich nicht unbillich die jenigen/ welchen dieses geringe Wercklein vorkommen wird/ verwundern/ worümb Ich als dem von E. Edlen/ WohlEhrnv. und Hochw. Rath allhier zu Leipzig vor 6. Jahren die *Directio Generalis* der Music in ihren Kirchen/ wie auch derselben *Informatio* in der Schul großgünstig auffgetragen/ mir vorgenommen/ mich mit einem weltlichen *Opere* zum erstenmal in öffentlichen Druck sehen zu lassen; da mir doch *Officii* wegen ein Geistliches Werck viel besser angestanden hätte. Dieselbigen aber sollen wissen/ daß dieses nicht neulich/ sondern vor langer Zeit schon verfertiget/ ja auch vor etlichen Jahren schon zum Druck hat sollen befördert werden/ worzwischen doch immer Hinderungen sich gefunden/ daß es nicht geschehen. Weil denn in demselbigen nichts ärgerliches/ sondern meistentheils allerhand lustige und possierliche *Inventiones* enthalten; und vor dessen meine Sel. Herren *Antecessores* dergleichen auch *ediret*; Habe ich auff guter und vornehmer Freunde Beyrathen solche hervor zu geben kein Bedencken mehr getragen.

Es seynd 20. Stück/ 10. Oden/ oder Canzonetten/ die übrige 10. sind theils Madrigalien/ theils nur *Epigrammata*, welche ich insgesammt Madrigalien genennet/

To the Reader.
Those persons who may get hold of this unimportant little work will, not unreasonably, wonder why I—as one whom the Right Noble, Very Reverend, and Very Wise Council of the city of Leipzig six years ago most favorably charged with the general direction of the music in its churches as well as the music instruction at school—have decided to present myself for the first time in public print with a secular opus, although ex officio, it would be more proper for me to publish a sacred work. Such persons should know, however, that the present work was not composed only recently; in fact, it was finished a long time ago and would have reached the press several years before now were it not for obstacles that prevented this from happening. And as it contains nothing offensive, but mostly consists of funny and droll inventions of all kinds, and because in former times my distinguished predecessors published similar things, following the council of good and noble friends I have not hesitated to publish it.

There are twenty pieces; ten are odes, or canzonettas; of the other ten some are madrigals, some mere epigrams. All of these latter I have called madrigals because in terms of their ratio formalis there is no great difference

weil unter einem *Epigrammate* und Madrigal, was ihre *rationem formalem* anbetrifft/ keine grosse *Differentz* ist/* und über dieses man einem *Epigrammati* in der Music eben so wohl die Art eines Madrigals geben kan/ als einem Madrigal selbst/ welches denen jenigen *Musicis* bewust/ so beydes versuchet. Es seynd aber die meisten/ als das 1. 2. 4. 5. 8. 11. 12. 14. 15. 18. und 20ste von Herr David Elias Heidenreichen/ als meinen sonderbahren guten Freunde erfunden worden/ die übrigen sind theils aus Hr. Georg Schochens/ theils aus anderer *Authorum* gedrückten *operibus* genommen. Und habe ich eine ziemliche Anzahl dergleichen Sachen noch bey mir/ welche künfftig/ dafern ich vermercke/ daß gegenwertige nicht unangenehm seyn werden/ auch ans Tageliecht kommen sollen.

Es soll aber mit allernechsten der Erste Theil meiner Geistlichen Concerten/ so von 1. 2. 3. 4. 5. und 6. Vocal= nebenst unterschiedlichen Instrumental=Stimmen (so auch zum Theil/ nach Belieben konnen ausgelassen werden/) nachfolgen. Und weil dieses gegenwertige Wercklein/ wie oben gemeldet/ schon vor etlichen Jahren verfertiget/ und (wie man im Sprichwort saget) *dies diem doceat*; Als bitte ich alle verständige *Musicos*, Sie wollen nicht so wohl aus diesem/ als aus zukünfftigen *operibus* das *judicium* von meiner geringen Erfahrenheit und Wissenschafft *in re Musicae* fällen/ und oberwähnte Geistliche Concerten mit nechsten gewiß erwarten.

*besiehe *Magn. Dn.* Casp. Zieglern von der Art und Eigenschafft eines Madrigals. *It. Lapinium in Instit. Lingv. Flor.*

between an epigram and a madrigal,* and because, moreover, an epigram can be set to music in the same way as a madrigal, as those musicians know who have tried both. Most of the pieces—numbers 1, 2, 4, 5, 8, 11, 12, 14, 15, 18, and 20—have texts by Mr. David Elias Heidenreich, a particularly good friend of mine; the remaining ones are set to texts taken from printed works by Georg Schoch and others. And I still have at hand a considerable number of similar pieces, which will also see the light of day should the present selection meet with a favorable reception.

But in the near future the first part of my sacred concertos for 1, 2, 3, 4, 5, and 6 voices and various instruments (some of which can be omitted if desired) is to follow. And because the present little work, as announced above, was written several years ago and, as the saying goes, dies diem doceat [= time will show], I would ask all the expert musicians not to pass judgment on my limited experience and expertise in re musicae on the basis of this and future works, but instead to expect the above-mentioned sacred concertos to appear soon.

* See Magn. Dn. Casp. Ziegler, "Concerning the Nature and Character of the Madrigal."[33] *It. Lapinium in Instit. Lingv. Flor.*

Notes

1. See Albert Göhler, *Verzeichnis der in den Frankfurter und Leipziger Messkatalogen der Jahre 1564 bis 1759 angezeigten Musikalien* (Leipzig 1902; reprint, Hilversum: Knufs, 1966), part 2, 45.

2. *Musicalisches Lexicon oder Musicalische Bibliothec* (Leipzig: Wolfgang Deer, 1732), 343.

3. *Denkmäler Deutscher Tonkunst*, vol. 58/59.

4. *Musikgeschichte Leipzigs*, vol. 2: *Von 1650 bis 1723* (Leipzig: Kistner & Siegel, 1926), especially 143 and 368–69.

5. See G. Tischer and K. Burchard, *Musikalienkatalog der Hauptkirche zu Sorau N./L.*, Beilage zu den Monatsheften für Musikgeschichte 1902.

6. See Elisabeth Noack, "Die Bibliothek der Michaeliskirche in Erfurt: Ein Beitrag zur Geschichte der musikalischen Formen und der Aufführungspraxis in der zweiten Hälfte des 17. Jahrhunderts," *Archiv für Musikwissenschaft* 7 (1925): 65–116, especially 65.

7. See H. J. Moser, *Corydon: Geschichte des mehrstimmigen Generalbaßliedes im deutschen Barock* (Braunschweig: Litolff, 1932), 1:vi and 18–23; 2:17–39.

8. "Nam et hic dicta Psalmorum, aliorumque librorum Bibliocorum optima notis Musicis adaptavit, tanta suavitate, tantaque artis praestantia." See Bernhard Friedrich Richter, "Zwei Funeralprogramme auf die Thomaskantoren Sebastian Knüpfer und Johann Schelle," *Monatshefte für Musikgeschichte* 33 (1901): 205–13, and 34 (1902): 9–16.

9. Johann Magnus Knüpfer was probably an important figure for the distribution of his father's works in middle Germany. He studied at Eisenach with Johann Christoph Bach and later became organist in Jena, where he instructed Johann Nikolaus Bach, the eldest son of his former teacher. In 1705, J. M. Knüpfer became organist at the Naumburg Wenzelskirche; he is also documented as court musician in Zeitz.

10. See the worklist by Arnold Schering in DDT, 58/59, xix–xxii; further titles of lost works occasionally show up in contemporary inventories. An up-to-date overview of the surviving sources for Knüpfer's compositions containing more than one voice can be found in Diane Parr Walker and Paul Walker, *German Sacred Polyphonic Vocal Music Between Schütz and Bach: Sources and Critical Editions*, Detroit Studies of Music Bibliography, no. 62 (Warren, Mich.: Harmonie Park Press, 1992), 202–6.

11. See Friedhelm Krummacher, "Zur Sammlung Jacobi der ehemaligen Fürstenschule Grimma," *Musikforschung* 16 (1963): 324–47.

12. See Gottfried Gille, "Der Kantaten-Textdruck von David Elias Heidenreich, Halle 1665, in den Vertonungen David Pohles, Sebastian Knüpfers, Johann Schelles und anderer: Zur Frühgeschichte der Concerto-Aria-Kantate," *Musikforschung* 38 (1985): 81–94.

13. Nine of them are listed by Gille, 91; the tenth piece is the anonymously transmitted fragment of "Die Liebe Gottes ist ausgegossen" in the Grimma Collection (D-Dlb, Mus. 2-E-557).

14. *M. MARTINI KEMPII | P. L. C. | Poetischer | Lust-Gedanken | Erster [Anderer] Theil . . . Jena/ druckts und verlegts Johann Jacob Bauhoffer/ Anno 1665* (copy at D-LEu, B.S.T. 8° 366). See also Karl Voßler, *Das deutsche Madrigal: Geschichte seiner Entwickelung bis in die Mitte des XVIII. Jahrhunderts* (Weimar: Felber, 1898), 58–62.

15. Cf. DDT, 58/59, xxii.

16. See Max Seiffert, "Die Chorbibliothek der St. Michaelis-schule in Lüneburg zu Seb. Bachs Zeit," *SIMG* 9 (1907/08): 593–621, especially 608, and DDT, 58/59, xxii.

17. S-Uu Vok. mus. i hs. 53:6. See Folke Lindberg, "Katalog över Dübensamlingen i Uppsala Universitets Bibliothek," unpublished manuscript dated 1947 in Uppsala Universitets-bibliothek, 226. The piece is listed as a sacred work in Walker and Walker, *German Sacred Polyphonic Vocal Music*, 205.

18. The piece was hitherto considered lost; the only known reference appeared in Walther's *Musicalisches Lexicon*. Recently, however, a copy of the print was discovered at the Thüringi-sche Landesbibliothek at Weimar (RISM A: K 1001a).

19. M. Meibom, *Antiquae musicae auctores septem* (Amsterdam: Ludwig Elzevir, 1652).

20. See *Die Musik in Geschichte und Gegenwart*, s.v. "Leipziger Musikhandschriften," by Peter Hauschild.

21. See Richter, "Zwei Funeralprogramme," 208–9.

22. Cf. Charton T. Lewis, *Elementary Latin Dictionary* (Oxford: Oxford University Press, 1891), 294.

23. For a general overview see Friedhelm Krummacher, *Die Überlieferung der Choralbearbeitungen in der frühen evangelischen Kantate: Untersuchungen zum Handschriftenrepertoire evangeli-scher Figuralmusik im späten 17. und beginnenden 18. Jahrhundert,* Berliner Studien zur Musikwissenschaft, 10 (Berlin: Merse-burger, 1965), passim.

24. See Moser, *Corydon*, passim.

25. See Werner Braun, *Die Musik des 17. Jahrhunderts*, Neues Handbuch der Musikwissenschaft, vol. 14 (Wiesbaden: Akademische Verlagsanstalt Athenaion, 1981), 142.

26. Ibid.

27. See Rudolf Gerber, preface to *Johann Jeep, Studen-tengärtlein (1605–1626),* Das Erbe deutscher Musik, Mehrstim-miges Lied, vol. 4 (Wolfenbüttel: Möseler, 1958), xii.

28. See Braun, *Die Musik des 17. Jahrhunderts,* 147.

29. See Moser, *Corydon,* 15.

30. On Heidenreich see Karl Goedeke, *Grundriß zur Geschichte der deutschen Dichtung,* vol. 3 (Dresden: Ehlermann, 1887), 221–22; Egbert Krispyn, "David Elias Heidenreich: Zur Biographie einer literarischen Randfigur," *Daphnis* 13 (1984): 275–98.

31. Based on biographical data provided by Manfred Lem-mer.

32. J. G. Schoch, *Neu=erbauter Poetischer Lust= und Blumen=Garten . . .* (Leipzig: Christian Kirchner, 1660), nos. LXXIII and XLIII.

33. See Caspar Ziegler, *Von den Madrigalen, Einer schönen und zur Musik bequemesten Art Verse Wie sie nach der Italiener Manier in unserer Deutschen Sprache auszuarbeiten Nebenst etlichen Exempeln* (Leipzig: Christian Kirchner, 1653). On Ziegler see Voßler, *Das deutsche Madrigal,* 43–50; and Philipp Spitta "Die Anfänge madrigalischer Dichtung in Deutsch-land," in his *Musikgeschichtliche Aufsätze* (Berlin: Paetel, 1894), 63–76.

Texts and Translations

The texts presented below are an accurate transcription of the original print, but in order to make the old German more comprehensible, the orthography and punctuation have been slightly modernized. All translations are by the editor.

1. Madrigale

Meer, Erd' und Sonne trinken,
es trinket Laub und Gras,
wer wird es uns denn wehren,
mit Trinken uns zu nähren?
Runda! Hier ist ein Glas!
Sa! In dem lieben Nassen
kann alles, was da lebet, Leben fassen.

David Elias Heidenreich

1. Madrigal

Sea, earth, and sun are constantly drinking,
so too are the leaves and grass;
who, then, would restrain us
from living upon drinking?
Runda! Here is a glass!
Sa! In the delightful wetness
all that lives can seize life.

2. Canzonetta

Ich sehne mich.
Ach! mein Augentrost,
du zart'ste Jungfer Blume,
nach deiner Schönheit Ruhme,
weil Amor sich erbost,
und mein sonst frank und frei Verlangen
nunmehr mit Krankheit hält umfangen.

Ich sehne mich.
Hilf, Schöne du!
Vergnüge meine Lüste
durch Augen, Mund, und Brüste,
ich schicke mich dazu.
Mein feuerheißes Liebesfieber,
das stillet sich durch nichts nicht lieber.

Ich sehne mich.
Ach! springt mir doch bei,
ihr Glieder meiner Schönen.
Vergnüget doch mein Sehnen,
ihr Arzt und Arzenei.
Hab ich ein bißchen euch zu Willen,
so wird sich bald mein Sehnen stillen.

David Elias Heidenreich

2. Canzonetta

I am yearning—
ah! you comfort of my eyes,
you most graceful Miss Flower—
for the praise of your beauty,
since Cupid grows angry
and my longing, formerly frank and free,
now embraces with distemper.

I am yearning,
help, Beauty as you are,
satisfy my desires
with eyes, mouth, and breasts,
I am resigned to them;
my love-fever, hot as fire,
will not be satisfied better than by this.

I am yearning,
ah! pray, assist me,
ye limbs of my Beauty.
Give pleasure to my longing,
you physician and physic (remedy),
if you are willing to assist a little,
then my desire will end soon.

3. Madrigale

Ade, du Tausendschatz,
ich kann um dich nicht weinen,
Ziehst du gleich itzt davon,
so weiß ich doch noch einen.

4. Canzonetta

Ei, Mädchen, nicht zu stolz!
Ich weiß, ihr müßt es mir gestehen,
daß ihr nicht könnt mit Holz
einmal zu Bette gehen.
Ihr seid kein Nönnchen nicht,
das seinen Schlafgesellen
läßt in dem Walde fällen.

Manch Mutter Kind, das muß
sich zwar in Einsamkeit verzehren,
und kostet keinen Kuß,
und lernet kein Vermehren.
Doch tät's das arme Ding,
wenn sich nur jemand fände,
der sie der Not entbände.

Ihr aber Mädchen seid
zu eurem auserlesnen Glücke
in einer bessern Zeit,
drum denket doch zurücke.
Greift wacker um euch zu,
ihr könnt's doch nicht entbehren,
was man euch will gewähren.

Kommt mir nur ja nicht mehr
mit solchen Fahrten aufgezogen,
ich geb euch kein Gehör,
und halt es für erlogen.
Wenn ihr euch künftig wehrt,
so will ich euch in Scherzen
noch fünfzigmal mehr herzen.

Spreizt, quickt und sperrt euch denn,
ich werde mich an nichts nicht kehren,
ich weiß schon wie und wenn,
und merke diese Lehren.
Die Mädchen stellen sich,
das Löffeln zu vermeiden,
da sie's doch gerne leiden.

David Elias Heidenreich

5. Madrigale

Kauft Rattenpulver! Mäusepulver!
Hier ist der Mann,
der sie vertreiben kann,
Er hilft vor Flöh' und Läuse,
vor Wanzgen, Ratten, Mäuse,
und was sonst mag für Ungeziefer sein,
doch nicht gezählt die bösen Weiber drein.

David Elias Heidenreich

3. Madrigal

Farewell, sweetheart of thousands!
I cannot weep for you,
even if you may now take your leave,
I still know somebody else.

4. Canzonetta

Ah, young Lady, do not be too haughty!
I know, you must confess to me,
that you can never go
to bed with a piece of wood.
You aren't a little nun
getting her bed-fellow by having
chopped him down in the forest.

Many a mother's daughter
must waste away in loneliness
and taste no kiss
and never learn to multiply.
But the poor little thing would do it
provided that there were anybody
to rescue her from all needs.

You, girls, however, are—
extremely luckily to you—
in a better period,
so you may recall this to your mind.
Lay hold of what is surrounding you,
you cannot miss
what one is willing to grant you.

Don't really tell me
things like that,
I won't give you any hearing
and consider it for false.
If you will resist in future,
then I would caress you just for the sport of it
fifty times more.

Even if you may strive and resist against it,
I shall not care for anything,
I already know the way and the time
and will bear in mind these lessons.
Girls only pretend
to shrink away from making love,
whereas they really like it.

5. Madrigal

Buy rat's and mouse's bane,
here is the man
who is able to banish them.
He will give you help against fleas and lice,
against bedbugs, rats, and mice,
and against all other vermin,
but not against shrews.

6. Canzonetta

Liesielis, ist denn dies gewiß,
daß ich um dich den Tag soll fliehen?
Ei nu, so tu' doch nur dies,
daß ich dich darf zu Nacht bemühen.
Liesielis, schläfst du denn schon,
höre! höre! Eh' der Ton
mir auf der Zunge gar vergehet;
sieh um dich, wer doch vor deinem Fenster stehet,

ängstiglich
und über sich
mit Tränen um Erbarmung flehet.

Ist vergünnt mir ein Seufzerwind?
Will ich ihn durch die Nacht dir schicken;
soll ich um dich, liebstes Kind,
aus mir die Seele seufzend drücken.
Liesielis, willst du denn dies?
Willst du? Willst du? Liesielis!
Ich werd' es dir nicht abschlagen.
Könnten wir auch lieben noch nach unsern Tagen,
wollt' ich hier
um die Revier
all' Abend kommen her zu klagen.

Aber, ach! viel Ungemach
erzähl' ich nur den bloßen Stufen.
Von ihr wird hier niemand wach,
doch halt, ich will noch einmal rufen.
Liesielis, schläfst du, mein Kind?
Schläfst du? Schläfst du? Ist vergünnt,
vor deiner Türe mir zu stehen?
Darf ich wohl so späte um Erbarmung flehen?
Traurens voll?
Sie schweigt, ich soll,
ich seh' es, von ihr weg nur gehen.

Johann Georg Schoch

7. Madrigale

Weg, Mars, mit deiner Faust!
Dein Krieg ist nicht vonnöten.
Der süße Venuskrieg,
der kann viel besser töten.

8. Canzonetta

Es muß in mir die Liebe quellen,
ein Mäulchen füllt mich täglich an.
Ihr, die ihr liebt,
und nur mit Hoffen euch betrübt,
besehet mich, was man mir hat getan.
Ist's nicht? Ich liebe recht mit Amabellen.

Kein Wirbelwind erreget Wellen
auf meiner stillen Liebessee,
und meiner Fahrt

6. Canzonetta

Liesielis, is it really true
that I shall shun the day because of you?
Now then, so do only this,
that I may bother you by night.
Liesielis, are you already sleeping?
Listen! Listen! Before the sound
will pass away from my tongue;
look around and see who is standing in front of your
     window
fearfully,
and for himself
is imploring for pity with tears.

May I be permitted to utter a sigh-breeze?
I will send it to you through the night;
shall I, sighing, about you, dearest child,
squeeze my soul out of myself?
Liesielis, do you really want this?
If you want it, Liesielis,
I will not refuse you.
If we could still love each other even after our days,
I would come hither
around this ground
in order to make laments all night.

But ah, much trouble
I am reporting merely to the steps.
From this will no one here awake,
but ho, I will call again.
Liesielis, are you asleep, my dear?
Do you sleep? May I be permitted
to stand in front of thy door?
May I pray for mercy so late,
full of grief?
She keeps silence, I should,
methinks, part from her.

7. Madrigal

Away, Mars, with your fist!
Your war is unnecessary.
It is the sweet Venus-war
which can kill much better.

8. Canzonetta

There must swell love within me,
a little mouth is filling me up day in, day out.
You who are in love
and are only afflicted through hoping,
look at me, what one did do to me.
Is it not so? I am well in love with Amabella.

There is no whirlwind causing waves
onto my calm love-sea,
and to my course

geschieht durch keiner Wetter Art,
noch sonst durch was auch im geringsten weh.
Ist's nicht? Ich liebe recht mit Amabellen.

Kein Neider kann mir was vergällen.
Ich bin zu tief gewurzelt ein.
Wagt einer sich,
und dichtet irgend was auf mich,
So kanns doch nicht im gringsten kräftig sein.
Ists nicht? Ich liebe recht mit Amabellen.

Es wirkt bei mir mehr als Morsellen,
wenn ich ihr Mündchen durch den Kuß
in Heimlichkeit
bei einer uns gelegnen Zeit
darf rühren an und das mit Überfluß.
Ists nicht? Ich liebe recht mit Amabellen.

Es schmecket mir als wie Morellen,
wenn von den Lippen ich den Saft
der Liebesgunst
mit einer zugelassnen Brunst
vertraulich und begierig aufgerafft.
Ists nicht? Ich liebe recht mit Amabellen.

Räumt mir nur ein dies Liebesquellen,
kein Mensche liebet mir doch gleich.
Weil nun aus mir
durch Küssen Liebe fleußt herfür,
und meinen Mund ein Mündchen machet reich,
daß ich gefunden nur bei Amabellen.

David Elias Heidenreich

through neither kind of tempest
nor anything else will in the least be done any harm.
Is it not so? I am well in love with Amabella.

There is no grudger who is able to embitter me in any way.
I am too deeply rooted.
If there is anybody venturing
to pacify me by anything,
it cannot in the least be too strong.
Is it not so? I am well in love with Amabella.

It has more effect on me than lozenges
when I her little mouth with a kiss
in secret
during a time convenient to both of us
may touch abundantly.
Is it not so? I am well in love with Amabella.

It tastes to me like morels
when I picked up from the lips
the liquor of love's favour
with an allowed ardour
intimately and with desire.
Is it not so? I am well in love with Amabella.

Concede me this fountain of love,
no other human being loves like me,
because from me
through kissing love is flowing,
and my mouth is being made rich by a little mouth
that I found only with Amabella.

9. Madrigale

Verzeiht mir, schönes Volk,
daß ich euch muß vergleichen
dem Miste vor der Tür,
denn dies ist euer Zeichen.
So nun der Mist und ihr sollt werden weggenommen,
so muß der Freiersmann und Kärner Geld bekommen.

9. Madrigal

Forgive me, pretty folk,
that I must compare you
with the dung lying in front of the door,
for this is your mark.
Now if both the dung and you are to be removed,
the wooer as well as the cart-man must be paid.

10. Canzonetta

O heller Glanz, du güldnes Licht,
komm, zeige dich doch mir,
ach! gönne mir dein Angesicht,
geh doch einmal herfür.
Laß auf dem Perlenwagen
am Himmel dich hertragen
du aller Sternen Zier.

O Fackel an der Stirnen Bau,
zu prangen aufgesteckt,
wenn ich nur deine Strahlen schau,
so ist mein Sinn verrückt,
so mächtig ist dein Blitzen,
daß ich fast nicht kann sitzen,
und deinem Brennen trau.

10. Canzonetta

O thou bright radiance, thou golden light,
come, present yourself to me,
ah! grant me your face,
appear at length.
Let carry yourself in the pearl-chaise
around the skies,
thou adornment of all stars.

O thou torch
being put upon the forehead in order to shine,
when I am only looking at your beams
my mind is getting crazy,
your glittering is so powerful
that I can hardly sit
and trust your burning.

Doch ohne dich nur einen Tag
zu leben ist zu schwer,
daß auch fast kaum der Atem mag
zuletzt sich regen mehr.
Wenn du dich hast verborgen,
so steh' ich stets in Sorgen
um deiner Strahlen Heer.

Ach! renne durch die güldne Bahn,
es ist ja hohe Zeit,
denn wenn du mich nicht blickest an,
so frißt mich Schmerz und Leid.
Du Säugamm' aller Sternen,
ach! laß doch nicht entfernen
dein Äuglein allzuweit.

But living without you only one day
is too difficult,
so that scarcely breath
may at last be stirring.
When you have hidden yourself
I am always in great pain
for the host of your beams.

Ah, do run through the golden orbit,
it is really high time,
for if you do not look at me
pain and grief will devour me.
Thou wet-nurse of all stars,
ah, let not withdraw too far
thy little eyes.

11. Madrigale

Dein Vater ist ein Schelm,
die Mutter aus der frechen Huren Orden,
und du auch selbst bist jüngst ein Hürchen worden;
das klingt fürwahr nicht fein.
Doch hast du viel Dublonen,
so will man deiner schonen,
du sollst hinfort ein ehrlich Mädchen sein.

David Elias Heidenreich

11. Madrigal

Your father is a scoundrel,
your mother one out of the cheeky order of whores,
and even yourself recently became a little harlot;
this does not sound nice indeed.
But if you have got many doubloons,
then you will be spared,
you are to be henceforth an honest girl.

12. Canzonetta

Wer durch die Schmeichelei
des Glückes was erlanget,
der bläst sich auf und pranget
und meinet, daß sein Gut
noch zweimal größer sei.
Doch mißt er durch ein falsches Maß.
Denn das bleibt wohl dabei,
Das Glücke trügt wie Glas.

Wer siehet nicht dafür,
wie er ins Unglück rennet,
und Schaden Vorteil nennet,
dieweil ein falscher Glanz
versperrt der Augen Tür.
Er liebt Gefahr ohn' Unterlaß.
Denn täglich hört mans schier,
das Glücke blend't wie Glas.

In solcher Zauberei,
so geht er denn zugrunde,
so läuft er nach dem Schlunde,
der alles in sich schlingt,
wie groß und reich es sei.
Denn Glück ist seines Unglücks Aas.
Und endlich bleibts dabei,
das Glücke bricht wie Glas.

David Elias Heidenreich

12. Canzonetta

He who has gained something
through adulation of fortune
puffs himself up and makes a show
and thinks his property
to be twice as much.
But he is measuring by a wrong measure.
For, as a matter of fact,
luck is as deceptive as glass.

He who does not look
to running into ill luck
and calling disadvantage an advantage,
because a false glitter
blocks up the eyes' door,
likes danger continually,
for day by day one can always learn
that luck is dazzling like glass.

In such an enchantment
he then goes to ruin
running into the gulf
which swallows everything
as big and rich as it may be.
For fortune is his misfortune's carrion.
And finally it is so:
Luck breaks like glass.

13. Madrigale

Schönheit, die ist sehr beliebet,
wo sie wahre Tugend und die Zucht zu Stützen hat.
Aber wo kein Geld dabei,
ist es lauter Phantasei.
Dieses alles fehlet dir,
gute Nacht! mit deiner Zier.

14. Canzonetta

Marindchen, mein Leben,
das lebet in mir;
sie hat mir gegeben,
ihr Herzchen voll Schmerzchen,
und voller Begier.
Da leb ich nun glücklich,
geschicklich,
und folge der Liebe bei ihrem Panier.

Das liebliche Kindchen,
das schickt sich zu mir.
Es gibt mir sein Mündchen,
das Schätzchen, voll Schmätzchen
und voller Begier.
Da küss' ich nun glücklich,
geschicklich,
und brauche des Purpurs geheiligte Zier.

Die Keusche, die Schöne,
die liebet mit mir.
Und wenn ich mich sehne,
so wachet und lachet
die fromme Begier.
Da lieb ich nun glücklich,
geschicklich,
und spüre kein besser Vergnügen allhier.
David Elias Heidenreich

15. Madrigale

O Scherschliep! Messerschliep!
Laßt eure Scheren schleifen,
so dürft ihr euch nicht um das Schneiden keifen.
Der ist ein armer Mann,
der scharf nicht schneiden kann.
David Elias Heidenreich

16. Canzonetta

Zerspalte dich, verführter Sinn.
Die Hoffnung ist dahin!
Sehr schlecht ist der Gewinn.
Im Lieben ist fürwahr allein
die größte Pein,
in Cloris Herz auch wohl selbdritte sein.

Was hilfts, ob sie gleich freundlich scheint,
Es kömmt ein ander Freund,

13. Madrigal

Beauty enjoys great favor
when supported by real virtue and chastity.
But where no money is present,
it is nothing but an illusion.
In all this you are wanting,
farewell with all your grace.

14. Canzonetta

It is little Marinda, my darling,
who lives in me;
she has given me
her little heart full of pains
and full of desire.
There I am now living in happiness
and cleverness
following love with its banner.

It is the lovely child
who suits me.
She gives me her little mouth,
this sweetheart, with smacks
and full of desire.
There I am now kissing in happiness
and cleverness
making use of the purple's godly grace.

It is the virtuous one, the beautiful one,
who loves together with me.
And when I am yearning,
then is watching and laughing
the pious desire.
There I am now loving in happiness
and cleverness
feeling no better pleasure here.

15. Madrigal

Oh shear-grinder! Knife-grinder!
Let your scissors grind,
and you may not worry about cutting.
He who cannot cut sharply
is a wretched man.

16. Canzonetta

Split yourself, seduced mind,
hope is gone!
So gain is very small.
The greatest pain in love
is indeed
to be only third in Cloris' heart.

Of what use is it if she seems to be friendly,
there comes another friend

mit dem sie's lieber meint.
Im Lieben ist fürwahr allein
die größte Pein,
in Cloris Herz auch wohl selbdritte sein.

Laß sie, und mach dich frei von ihr.
Mein Herze folge mir:
Sie hälts nicht recht mit dir.
So bist du frei von solcher Pein
und kannst allein
der lieben Marilis ganz eigen sein.

17. Madrigale

Es will die Galathee
sich hoch und teu'r vermessen,
und schwöret Stein und Bein,
sie habe nie gesessen
dort bei dem Corydon.
Der Daphnis gläubt es nicht
und sagt ihr ins Gesicht:
Es wäre doch geschehn.
Drum will sie mit ihm wetten
um eine Tonnen Golds,
auch um drei güldne Ketten
und einen Demantring,
viel Perlen noch dazu.
Ei mein! Sie hat gewiß
mehr Geld als ich und du.

18. Canzonetta

Melinde, du bist hart
und unbarmherzig in der Liebe.
Dein Herz ist ganz erstarrt
und fühlet keine Seelentriebe.
Drum komm ich auch so sehr in Not
und fühle nichts als nur den Tod.

Ach! könnte doch dein Geist
dein marmelsteinern Herz erweichen,
das nichts in sich beschleust,
als strengen Mut und seinesgleichen;
so würde mich die harte Not
nicht führen hin bis in den Tod.

Ach! fange doch nur an,
dich über mich einst zu erbarmen.
So ist schon viel getan,
dadurch du retten kanst mich Armen,
und meine Last der harten Not,
die drückt mich nicht bis in den Tod.

Du wirst hernach den Schmerz
sowohl als ich bei dir empfinden,
und dein itzt steinern Herz
wird Fleisch und Blut und Liebe finden,
du wirst es sehn, wie groß die Not,
und wie ich schon sei lebend tot.

whom she is more fond of.
The greatest pain in love
is indeed
to be only third in Cloris' heart.

Let her go and get rid of her,
my heart, follow me:
She is not fair with you.
So you are free from pain like that,
and you may alone
belong entirely to dear Marilis.

17. Madrigal

It is Galathea
presuming solemnly
and swearing blind
that she never sat there
with Corydon.
Daphnis does not believe it
and tells her to her face
that it did happen.
Therefore she wants to make a bet with him
for a ton of gold,
also for three golden chains
as well as a diamond-ring
and many pearls besides that.
Dear me! She owns, no doubt,
more money than you and me.

18. Canzonetta

Melinda, you are cruel
and ruthless in love.
Your heart is totally numb
and does not feel any motion of the soul.
Therefore I am getting so much in trouble
feeling nothing but death.

Ah, if only your mind
could soften your marble heart,
which does not include anything
but rigorous mettle and the like;
so hard distress
would not take me to death.

Ah, do really begin
to show mercy to me some day.
Then much would have already been done
through which you can rescue me, wretched as I am,
and my burden of hard distress
does not squeeze me to death.

You will afterwards feel the pain,
as I do, for yourself,
and your heart, at present as hard as stone,
will find flesh, and blood, and love.
You will see how hard distress can be,
and how I, though still alive, am already dead.

Wo du ein Mensche bist,
so kannst du nicht stets grausam bleiben.
Du mußt, was grausam ist,
aus deiner holden Brust vertreiben.
Erbarmst du dich denn meiner Not,
so lieben wir bis in den Tod.

David Elias Heidenreich

If you are a human being,
then you cannot always keep cruel.
You must all that is cruel
banish from your charming breast.
If you will show mercy to my pains
then we love each other beyond the grave.

19. Madrigale

O wunderschönes Bild,
du Zwingerin des Herzen,
das du verwundet hast
durch deiner Liebe Pfeil.
Drum mache wiederum
auch meine Wunden heil.
Ich habe ja von dir
bekommen diesen Schmerzen.

19. Madrigal

Oh lovely image,
thou conqueror of the heart
which you have wounded
through the arrow of your love.
Therefore do heal up again
my wounds, too;
for I have been given
these pains from your side.

20. Canzonetta

Ihr Sorgen weicht!
Ihr Mörder meines Lebens!
Es ist vergebens,
daß man um euch die Backen bleicht.
Je mehr man sinnt und denket,
je mehr das Leben wird gekränket.

Ich mag mir nicht
mein Herze selber fressen.
Und wills vergessen,
wenn mir zuzeiten was gebricht.
Und soll ich gar nichts haben,
so werd' ich arm einmal begraben.

Wer kann die Pracht
nach seinem Tode spüren,
den Sarg zu zieren,
und was man sonst für Wesen macht?
Nur ehrlich sich verhalten,
das and're mag das Glücke walten.

Ein solcher Mut
ist stets bei sich vergnüget;
wie's auch sich füget.
Er bleibet groß, wie klein sein Gut.
Und ist ihm was bescheret,
so wirds ohn' das ihm nicht verwehret.

Weicht dann hinweg
ihr ungeheuren Sorgen.
Kein ein'ger Morgen
bringt mich durch euch zu meinem Zweck.
Wer Unglück will ertragen,
der muß sich eurer ganz entschlagen.

David Elias Heidenreich

20. Conzonetta

Ye sorrows, give way,
ye murderers of my life!
It is in vain
that one turns to death because of you.
The more one is meditating and thinking,
the more life is going to get mortified.

I have no mind
to eat my own heart up,
and I will forget it
if I am sometimes wanting anything.
And if I should not gain anything at all,
then I will once be buried in poverty.

Who may feel splendour
after death
by adorning the coffin
or else making much ado?
One must only behave honestly,
the rest luck may bring about.

A spirit like that
is always cheerful
whatever may happen.
He remains great, as small as his goods may be.
And if he will gain anything,
then he will not be prevented from it anyway.

Give way then,
ye monstrous sorrows.
Not a single morning
will bring me through yourselves to my end.
He who wants to bear misfortune
must totally banish you.

Sebastian Knüpffers
Lustige
Madrigalien und
Canzonetten/
und zwar
Die Madrigalien seynd von 4. 3.
und 2. Vocal-Stimmen alleine; Die
Canzonetten aber von 3.2. und einer Vocal-nebenst
beygefügten Instrumental-
Stimmen.

Bassus Continuus.

Leipzig/
In Verlegung des Authoris,
und bey Christian Kirchnern/Buchhändl. zu finden.

Gedruckt bey Johann-Erich Hahn/1663.

Plate 1. Title page of *Lustige Madrigalien und Canzonetten*, basso continuo partbook (courtesy Allgemeine Musikgesellschaft, Zurich)

Dem WohlEhrnvesten / HochAchtbarn
und Wohlgelahrten

Herrn CHRISTIANO PHILIPPI,
Jur. Utr. Candidato,

Meinem vielgünstigen und geehrten Freunde.

WOhlEhrnvester / HochAchtbahrer und
Wohlgelährter Herr / Die grossen Wolthaten
Seines tit. Magn. Herrn Vaters / als meines Großgünstigen
und Hochgeehrten Herrn Gevatters / Patroni und mächtigen Be-
förderers / welche ich / so lang ich in Leipzig gewesen / unwürdig ge-
nossen / verbinden mich / wo nicht zu einer Unmögligkeit / zum we-
nigsten doch zu einer derselben schuldigsten und danckbarlichen Erkäntnüß. Solche
aber in etwas nur zu beweisen / habe ich ietzund bey Ausfertigung dieses geringen
Musicalischen Wercfleins einige Gelegenheit an die Hand bekommen / welches dem
Herrn / als Einem sonderbahren Liebhaber der Music / wie auch dieser Edlen Kunst
ziemlichen theils Erfahrnen / so wohl oberregter Ursachen / als auch unserer beyden
nunmehro viel Jahr her gepflognen Freundschafft wegen Ich hiermit zugeschrieben
und offeriret haben will / dienstschuldigst bittend / Er wolle solches als eine Bezeigung
meines schuldigst danckbahren Gemüthes annehmen / und ferner in seine Freundschafft und Gunst lassen eingeschlossen seyn.

Gegeben in Leipzig den 9. Maji /
Anno 1663.

Seinen

Dienstschuldigsten

Sebastian Knüpffern /
Directorem der Music.

A ij   An

Plate 2. Dedication to Christian Philippi, basso continuo partbook, fol. 2r
(courtesy Allgemeine Musikgesellschaft, Zurich)

An den Leſer.

ES werden ſich nicht unbillich die jenigen/ welchen dieſes geringe Wercklein vorkommen wird/ verwundern/ worůmb Ich als dem von E. Edlen/ Wohl Ehrnv. und Hochw. Rath allhier zu Leipzig vor 6. Jahren die Directio Generalis der Muſic in ihren Kirchen/ wie auch derſelben Informatio in der Schul großgůnſtig auffgetragen/ mir vorgenommen/ mich mit einem weltlichen Opere zum erſtenmal in öffentlichen Druck ſehen zu laſſen; da mir doch Officii wegen ein Geiſtliches Werck viel beſſer angeſtanden hätte. Dieſelbigen aber ſollen wiſſen/ daß dieſes nicht neulich / ſondern vor langer Zeit ſchon verfertiget/ ja auch vor etlichen Jahren ſchon zum Druck hat ſollen befördert werden/ worzwiſchen doch immer Hinderungen ſich gefunden/ daß es nicht geſchehen. Weil denn in demſelbigen nichts ärgerliches/ ſondern meiſtentheils allerhand luſtige und poſſierliche Inventiones enthalten; und vor deſſen meine Sel. Herren Anteceſloresdergleichen auch ediret;. Habe ich auff guter und vornehmer Freunde Beyrathen ſolche hervor zu geben kein Bedencken mehr getragen.

Es ſeynd 20. Stück/ 10. Oden/ oder Canzonetten/ die übrige 10. ſind theils Madrigalien/ theils nur Epigrammata. welche ich ingeſamt Madrigalie genennet/ weil unter einem Epigrammate uñ Madrigal/ was ihre rationem formalem anbetrifft/ keine groſſe Differentz iſt/ †und über dieſes man einem Epigrammati in der Muſic eben ſo wohl die Art eines Madrigals geben kan/ als einem Madrigal ſelbſt/ welches denen jenigen Muſicis bewuſt/ ſo beydes verſuchet. Es ſeynd aber die meiſten/ als das 1. 2. 4. 5. 8. 11. 12. 14. 15. 18. und 20ſte von Herr David Elias Heidenreichen/

als

† beſiehe *Magn. Dn. Caſp. Zieglern von der Art und Eigenſchafft eines Madrigals.*
It, Lapinium in Inſtit Lingv. Flor.

Plate 3. Knüpfer's preface, basso continuo partbook, fol. 2v (courtesy Allgemeine Musikgesellschaft, Zurich)

als meinen sonderbahren guten Freunde erfunden worden/die ü-
brigen sind theils aus Hr. Georg Schochens/theils aus anderer
Authorum gedrückten operibus genommen. Vnd habe ich eine ziemliche Anzahl dergleichen Sachen noch bey mir / welche
künfftig/dafern ich vermercke / daß gegenwertige nicht unangenehm seyn werden/auch ans Tageliecht kommen sollen.

Es soll aber mit allernechsten der Erste Theil meiner
Geistlichen Concerten/so von 1. 2. 3. 4. 5. und 6. Vocal- nebenst unterschiedlichen Instrumental-Stimmen (so auch zum
Theil/nach Belieben konnen ausgelassen werden/) nachfolgen.
Vnd weil dieses gegenwertige Wercklein / wie oben gemeldet/
schon vor etlichen Jahren verfertiget/und (wie man im Sprichwort saget) dies diem docet; Als bitte ich alle verständige
Musicos, Sie wollen nicht so wohl aus diesem/als aus zukünfftigen operibus das judicium von meiner geringen Erfahrenheit
und Wissenschafft in re Musicâ fällen / und oberwähnte
Geistliche Concerten mit nechsten
gewiß erwarten.

Plate 4. Knüpfer's preface, basso continuo partbook, fol. 3r (courtesy Allgemeine Musikgesellschaft, Zurich)

, *fama KNûPFFERE vadum suavissime*
  tenta,
    Atqve hos in vulgus carminis ede modos.
*Si qvis erit, bibulus qvi dictitet auribus aptos,**
    Esse Mathematicos qvi ferat, alter erit.
Interea sacros concinna lætus ad usus,
    Qveis templa Harmoniis nostra animare soles.
Orpheus sic alter nobis diceris erisqve:
    Ille prius lapides, mox movet ille deos.

* Aristoteles Muſicam aliam Mathematicam, aliam
  Practicam & vulgarem facit. Ἁρμονικὴ ἥτε
  μαθηματικὴ.ἡ,ἡ καὶ ἡ κατὰ τὴ ἀκοήν. I. POST, A.
  nalyt, c.10.

                    Amico & Compatri honoratissimo
                              fac.
              FRID. RAPPOLT, POES. Prof:Publ.

Sonnet.

LAß/Edle Linden-Stadt / die lieben Alten preisen
    Orlanden Himmel-hoch/ und ihren Creqvillon/
    Und andre/welche sind belobt vom Singe-Thon.
Sieh deinen Knüpffer an! Er kan dein Orpheus heisen.

                                        Und

Plate 5. Eulogies on Knüpfer, basso continuo partbook, fol. 3v (courtesy Allgemeine Musikgesellschaft, Zurich)

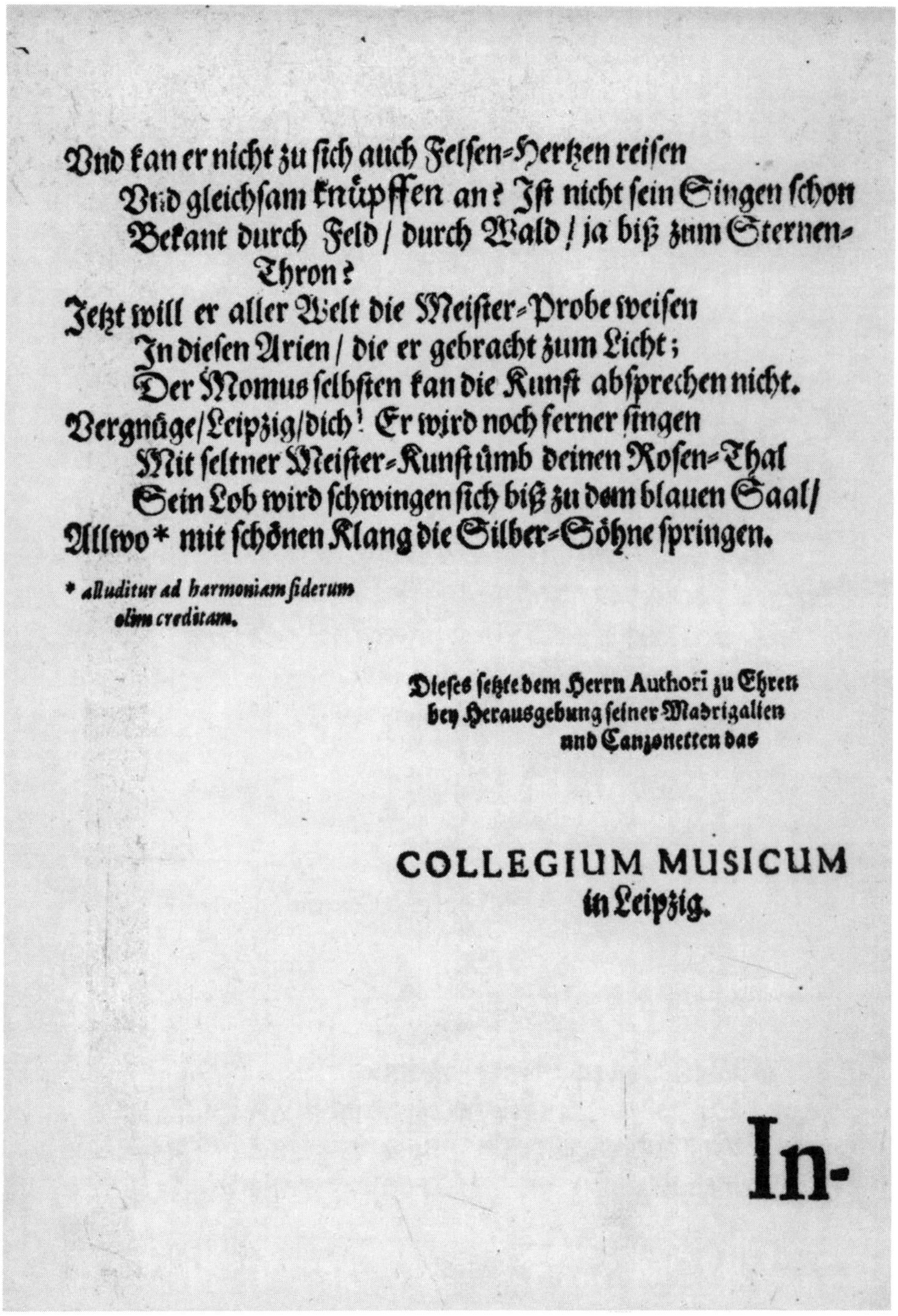

Vnd kan er nicht zu sich auch Felsen-Hertzen reisen
    Vnd gleichsam knüpffen an? Jst nicht sein Singen schon
    Bekant durch Feld/ durch Wald/ ja biß zum Sternen-
    Thron?
Jetzt will er aller Welt die Meister-Probe weisen
    In diesen Arien/ die er gebracht zum Licht;
    Der Momus selbsten kan die Kunst absprechen nicht.
Vergnüge/Leipzig/dich! Er wird noch ferner singen
    Mit seltner Meister-Kunst ümb deinen Rosen-Thal
    Sein Lob wird schwingen sich biß zu dem blauen Saal/
Allwo * mit schönen Klang die Silber-Söhne springen.

* alluditur ad harmoniam siderum
  olim creditam.

Dieses setzte dem Herrn Authori zu Ehren
bey Herausgebung seiner Madrigalien
und Canzonetten das

COLLEGIUM MUSICUM
in Leipzig.

In-

Plate 6. Eulogies on Knüpfer, basso continuo partbook, fol. 4r (courtesy All-gemeine Musikgesellschaft, Zurich)

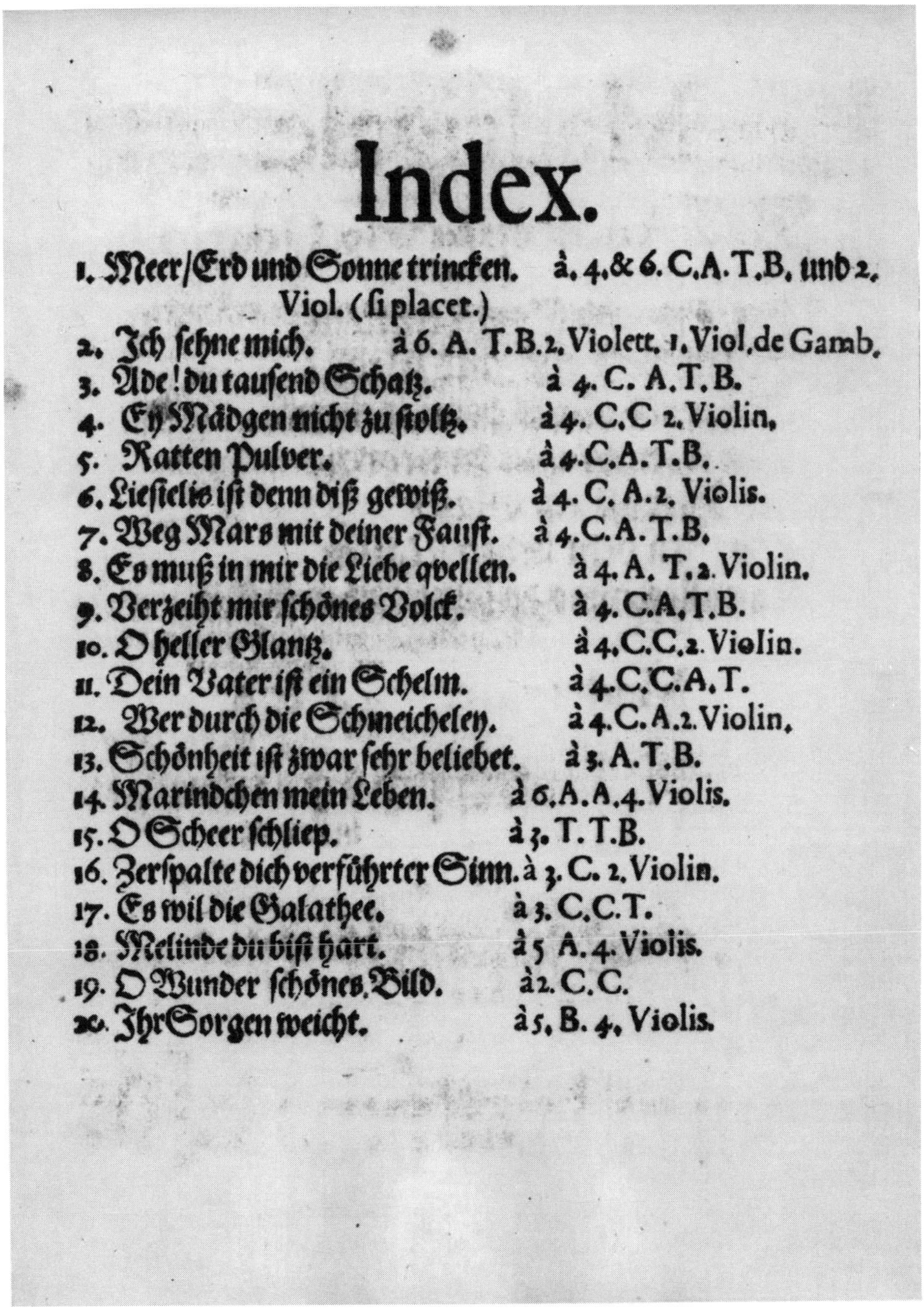

Index.

1. Meer/Erd und Sonne trincken. à. 4.& 6. C.A.T.B. und 2. Viol. (si placet.)
2. Ich sehne mich. à 6. A. T.B.2. Violett. 1. Viol.de Gamb.
3. Ade! du tausend Schatz. à 4. C. A.T.B.
4. Ey Mädgen nicht zu stoltz. à 4. C.C 2. Violin.
5. Ratten Pulver. à 4.C.A.T.B.
6. Lieselis ist denn diß gewiß. à 4. C. A. 2. Violis.
7. Weg Mars mit deiner Faust. à 4.C.A.T.B.
8. Es muß in mir die Liebe qvellen. à 4. A. T. 2. Violin.
9. Verzeiht mir schönes Volck. à 4. C.A.T.B.
10. O heller Glantz. à 4.C.C.2. Violin.
11. Dein Vater ist ein Schelm. à 4.C.C.A.T.
12. Wer durch die Schmeicheley. à 4.C.A.2.Violin.
13. Schönheit ist zwar sehr beliebet. à 3. A.T.B.
14. Marindchen mein Leben. à 6.A.A.4.Violis.
15. O Scheer schliep. à 3. T.T.B.
16. Zerspalte dich verführter Sinn. à 3. C. 2. Violin.
17. Es wil die Galathee. à 3. C.C.T.
18. Melinde du bist hart. à 5 A. 4. Violis.
19. O Wunder schönes Bild. à 2. C.C.
20. Ihr Sorgen weicht. à 5. B. 4. Violis.

Plate 7. Index, basso continuo partbook, fol. 4v (courtesy Allgemeine Musikgesellschaft, Zurich)

Plate 8. Beginning of no. 1, basso continuo partbook, fol. 5r (courtesy Allgemeine Musikgesellschaft, Zurich)

1. Madrigale

Meer, Erd' und Sonne trinken

Nach Anacreontis 19. Odario
David Elias Heidenreich

2

4

6

mit Trin- ken, mit Trin- ken uns zu __ näh- ren?

- ken, mit Trin- ken uns zu näh- ren?

- ken, mit Trin- ken uns zu näh- ren?

mit Trin- ken, mit Trin- ken uns zu näh- ren?

Sonata (se piace)
Allegro

Vn. 1

Vn. 2

B.c.

-da, run-da, run-da, run- da- di- nel- lu- la! Run- da- di- nel- lu- la! Sa, sa, sa, sa!

-da, run-da, run-da, run- da- di- nel- lu- la! Run- da- di- nel- lu- la! Sa, sa, sa, sa, sa, sa, sa, sa!

-da, run-da, run-da, run- da- di- nel- lu- la! Run- da- di- nel- lu- la! Sa, sa, sa, sa, sa, sa, sa, sa!

-da, run-da, run-da, run- da- di- nel- lu- la! Run- da- di- nel- lu- la! Sa, sa, sa, sa!

2. Canzonetta

Ich sehne mich

David Elias Heidenreich

18

2. Ich sehne mich.
   Hilf, Schöne du!
   Vergnüge meine Lüste,
   durch Augen, Mund, und Brüste,
   ich schicke mich dazu.
   Mein feuerheißes Liebesfieber,
   das stillet sich durch nichts nicht lieber.

3. Ich sehne mich.
   Ach! springt mir doch bei,
   ihr Glieder meiner Schönen.
   Vergnüget doch mein Sehnen,
   ihr Arzt und Arzenei.
   Hab ich ein bißchen euch zu Willen,
   so wird sich bald mein Sehnen stillen.

3. Madrigale

Ade, du Tausendschatz

22

4. Canzonetta

Ei, Mädchen, nicht zu stolz!

David Elias Heidenreich

-ge- sel- len läßt in dem Wal-
-sel- len läßt in dem Wal- - de ___

-de fäl- len, ihr seid kein
fäl- len,

Nönn- chen nicht, das sei- nen Schlaf- - ge- sel- len,
ihr seid kein Nönn- chen nicht, das sei- nen Schlaf- ge- - sel- len,

2. Manch Mutter Kind, das muß
sich zwar in Einsamkeit verzehren,
und kostet keinen Kuß,
und lernet kein Vermehren.
Doch tät's das arme Ding,
wenn sich nur jemand fände,
der sie der Not entbände.

3. Ihr aber Mädchen seid
zu eurem auserlesnen Glücke
in einer bessern Zeit,
drum denket doch zurücke.
Greift wacker um euch zu,
ihr könnt's doch nicht entbehren,
was man euch will gewähren.

4. Kommt mir nur ja nicht mehr
mit solchen Fahrten aufgezogen,
ich geb euch kein Gehör,
und halt es für erlogen.
Wenn ihr euch künftig wehrt,
so will ich euch in Scherzen
noch fünfzigmal mehr herzen.

5. Spreizt, quickt und sperrt euch denn,
ich werde mich an nichts nicht kehren,
ich weiß schon wie und wenn,
und merke diese Lehren.
Die Mädchen stellen sich,
das Löffeln zu vermeiden,
da sie's doch gerne leiden.

33

34

6. Canzonetta

Liesielis, ist denn dies gewiß

Johann Georg Schoch

2. Ist vergünnt mir ein Seufzerwind?
    Will ich ihn durch die Nacht dir schicken;
    soll ich um dich, liebstes Kind,
    aus mir die Seele seufzend drücken.
    Liesielis, willst du denn dies?
    Willst du? Willst du? Liesielis!
    Ich werd' es dir nicht abeschlagen.
    Könnten wir auch lieben noch nach unsern Tagen,
    wollt' ich hier
    um die Revier
    all' Abend kommen her zu klagen.

3. Aber, ach! viel Ungemach
    erzähl' ich nur den bloßen Stufen.
    Von ihr wird hier niemand wach,
    doch halt, ich will noch einmal rufen.
    Liesielis, schläfst du, mein Kind?
    Schläfst du? Schläfst du? Ist vergünnt,
    vor deiner Türe mir zu stehen?
    Darf ich wohl so späte um Erbarmung flehen?
    Trauerns voll?
    Sie schweigt, ich soll,
    ich seh' es, von ihr weg nur gehen.

7. Madrigale

Weg, Mars, mit deiner Faust

46

8. Canzonetta

Es muß in mir die Liebe quellen

David Elias Heidenreich

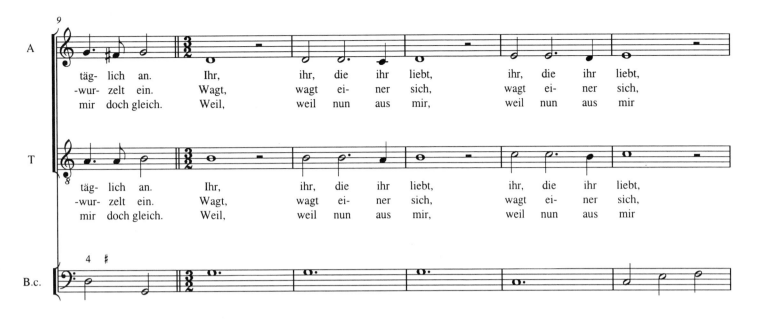

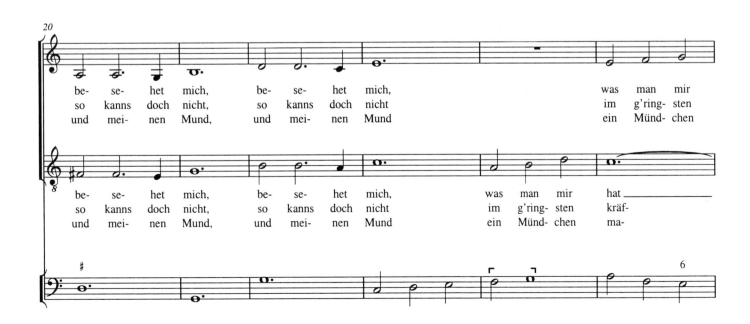

[fine]

9. Madrigale

Verzeiht mir, schönes Volk

54

10. Canzonetta

O heller Glanz

60

-rückt, so mäch-tig ist dein Blit- zen, daß ich fast nicht kann sit- zen,

-rückt, so mäch-tig ist dein Blit- zen, daß ich fast nicht kann sit- zen, und dei-nem

Vn. 1

Vn. 2

C 1
und dei-nem Bren- nen trau, so mäch-tig ist dein

C 2
Bren- nen trau, so mäch-tig ist dein Blit- zen,

B.c

Blit- zen, daß ich fast nicht kann sit- zen, und dei-nem Bren- nen trau.

daß ich fast nicht kann sit- zen, und dei-nem Bren- nen trau.

64

68

11. Madrigale

Dein Vater ist ein Schelm

David Elias Heidenreich

71

72

12. Canzonetta

Wer durch die Schmeichelei

David Elias Heidenreich

Wer durch die Schmei-che-lei des Glü-ckes was er- lan- get, der

Wer durch die Schmei-che-lei des Glü-ckes was er- lan- get,

2. Wer siehet nicht dafür,
   wie er ins Unglück rennet,
   und Schaden Vorteil nennet,
   dieweil ein falscher Glanz
   versperrt der Augen Tür.
   Er liebt Gefahr ohn' Unterlaß.
   Denn täglich hört mans schier,
   das Glücke blend't wie Glas.

3. In solcher Zauberei,
   so geht er denn zugrunde,
   so läuft er nach dem Schlunde,
   der alles in sich schlingt,
   wie groß und reich es sei.
   Denn Glück ist seines Unglücks Aas.
   Und endlich bleibts dabei,
   das Glücke bricht wie Glas.

13. Madrigale

Schönheit ist zwar sehr beliebet

14. Canzonetta

Marindchen, mein Leben

David Elias Heidenreich

2. Das liebliche Kindchen,
   das schickt sich zu mir.
   Es gibt mir sein Mündchen,
   das Schätzchen, voll Schmätzchen
   und voller Begier.
   Da küss' ich nun glücklich,
   geschicklich,
   und brauche des Purpurs geheiligte Zier.

3. Die Keusche, die Schöne,
   die liebet mit mir.
   Und wenn ich mich sehne,
   so wachet und lachet
   die fromme Begier.
   Da lieb ich nun glücklich,
   geschicklich,
   und spüre kein besser Vergnügen allhier.

15. Madrigale

O Scherschliep! Messerschliep!

David Elias Heidenreich

92

16. Canzonetta

Zerspalte dich, verführter Sinn

Johann Georg Schoch

schlecht ist der _____ Ge- winn. Im Lie- ben

ist für- wahr al- lein die größ- te Pein,

in Clo- ris Herz auch wohl selb- drit- te sein.

2. Was hilfts, ob sie gleich freundlich scheint,
es kömmt ein ander Freund,
mit dem sie's lieber meint.
Im Lieben ist füwahr allein
die größte Pein,
in Cloris Herz auch wohl selbdritte sein.

3. Laß sie, und mach dich frei von ihr.
Mein Herze folge mir:
Sie hälts nicht recht mit dir.
So bist du frei von solcher Pein,
und kannst allein
der lieben Marilis ganz eigen sein.

17. Madrigale

Es will die Galathee

19

-sicht: Es wä- re doch ge- schehn. Der Daph- nis gläubt es nicht, der

22

Daph- nis gläubt es nicht und sagt ihr ins Ge-sicht, es wä- re doch ge-schehn, und

25

Es will die Ga- la- thee sich

Es will die Ga- la-

sagt ihr ins Ge-sicht, es wä- re doch ge-schehn.

102

104

106

18. Canzonetta

Melinde, du bist hart

David Elias Heidenreich

Drum komm' ich auch so ___ sehr in Not und füh- le nichts als ___ nur den Tod,

drum komm' ich auch so ___ sehr in Not und füh- le nichts als ___ nur den Tod.

2. Ach! könnte doch dein Geist
   dein marmelsteinern Herz erweichen,
   das nichts in sich beschleußt,
   als strengen Mut und seinesgleichen;
   so würde mich die harte Not
   nicht führen hin bis in den Tod.

3. Ach! fange doch nur an,
   dich über mich einst zu erbarmen.
   So ist schon viel getan,
   dadurch du retten kannst mich Armen,
   und meine Last der harten Not,
   die drückt mich nicht bis in den Tod.

4. Du wirst hernach den Schmerz
   sowohl als ich bei dir empfinden,
   und dein itzt steinern Herz
   wird Fleisch und Blut und Liebe finden,
   du wirst es sehn, wie groß die Not,
   und wie ich schon sei lebend tot.

5. Wo du ein Mensche bist,
   so kannst du nicht stets grausam bleiben.
   Du mußt, was grausam ist,
   aus deiner holden Brust vertreiben.
   Erbarmst du dich denn meiner Not,
   so lieben wir bis in den Tod.

19. Madrigale

O wunderschönes Bild

116

20. Canzonetta

Ihr Sorgen, weicht!

David Elias Heidenreich

118

euch die Ba- - cken bleicht.

Je mehr man sinnt und den- ket, je mehr das

2. Ich mag mir nicht
mein Herze selber fressen.
Und wills vergessen,
wenn mir zuzeiten was gebricht.
Und soll ich gar nichts haben,
so werd' ich arm einmal begraben.

3. Wer kann die Pracht
nach seinem Tode spüren,
den Sarg zu zieren,
und was man sonst für Wesen macht?
Nur ehrlich sich verhalten,
das andre mag das Glücke walten.

4. Ein solcher Mut
ist stets bei sich vergnüget;
wie's auch sich füget.
Er bleibet groß, wie klein sein Gut.
Und ist ihm was bescheret,
so wirds ohn' das ihm nicht verwehret.

5. Weicht dann hinweg,
ihr ungeheuren Sorgen.
Kein ein'ger Morgen
bringt mich durch euch zu meinem Zweck.
Wer Unglück will ertragen,
der muß sich euer ganz entschlagen.

Critical Report

Sources

The Original Print (RISM A/I: K 1000)

Title page (see plate 1): *Sebastian Knüpffers | Lustige | Madrigalien und | Canzonetten/ | und zwar | Die Madrigalien seynd von 4. 3. | und 2. Vocal=Stimmen alleine; Die | Canzonetten aber von 3. 2. und einer Vocal= nebenst | beygefügten Instrumental = | Stimmen. | Prima [Secunda etc.] Vox. | [vignette] | Leipzig/ | In Verlegung des Authoris, | und bey Christian Kirchnern/ Buchhändl. zu finden. | Gedruckt bey Johann Erich Hahn/ 1663.*

Seven partbooks, printed in movable type and with ornamental initials featuring the first letter of the pertinent texts. Only the *Bassus Continuus* partbook includes the dedication to Christian Philippi (plate 2), Knüpfer's preface (plates 3–4), and eulogies on Knüpfer (plates 5–6). Each partbook contains on fol. 1r a title page (see above) and on fol. 1v (*Bassus Continuus*, fol. 4v) a standardized index, indicating title, number of voices and scoring (plate 7):

1. Meer/ Erd und Sonne trincken.	à 4. & 6. C. A. T. B. und 2. Viol. (si placet.)
2. Ich sehne mich.	à 6. A. T. B. 2. Violett. 1. Viol. de Gamb.
3. Ade! du tausend Schatz.	à 4. C. A. T. B.
4. Ey Mädgen nicht zu stoltz.	à 4. C. C. 2. Violin.
5. Ratten Pulver.	à 4. C. A. T. B.
6. Liesielis ist denn diß gewiß.	à 4. C. A. 2. Violis.
7. Weg Mars mit deiner Faust.	à 4. C. A. T. B.
8. Es muß in mir die Liebe qvellen.	à 4. A. T. 2. Violin.
9. Verzeiht mir schönes Volck.	à 4. C. A. T. B.
10. O heller Glantz.	à 4. C. C. 2. Violin.
11. Dein Vater ist ein Schelm.	à 4. C. C. A. T.
12. Wer durch die Schmeicheley.	à 4. C. A. 2. Violin.
13. Schönheit ist zwar sehr beliebet.	à 3. A. T. B.
14. Marindchen mein Leben.	à 6. A. A. 4. Violis.
15. O Scheer schliep.	à 3. T. T. B.
16. Zerspalte dich verführter Sinn.	à 3. C. 2. Violin.
17. Es wil die Galathee.	à 3. C. C. T.
18. Melinde du bist hart.	à 5. A. 4. Violis.
19. O Wunder schönes Bild.	à 2. C. C.
20. Ihr Sorgen weicht.	à 5. B. 4 Violis.

Within the partbooks each composition bears a number and a caption title indicating in varying accuracy its genre and the number of parts and voice types employed. The contents of each individual part is listed below:

Bassus Continuus. Title page (fol. 1r); dedication: "Dem WohlEhrnvesten/ HochAchtbarn | und Wohlgelahrten | Herrn CHRISTIANO PHILIPPI" (fol. 2r); preface: "An den Leser" (fols. 2v–3r); eulogies by Friedrich Rappolt and the "COLLEGIUM MUSICUM | in Leipzig" (fols. 3v–4r); index (fol. 4v); music (fols. 5r–22v); errata (fol. 23). For four madrigals (nos. 1, 5, 11, and 15) the entire text is given preceding the respective music (cf., plate 8).

Instrumentum Primum. Title page (fol. 1r); index (fol. 1v); music (fols. 2r–8v). *Violino 1,* nos. 1 (*se piace*), 4, 8, 10, 12, 16; *Violetta 1,* no. 2; *Viola de Braz. 1,* no. 6; *Viola 1,* nos. 14, 18, 20.

Instrumentum Secundum. Title page (fol. 1r); index (fol. 1v); music (fols. 2r–8v). *Violino 2,* nos. 1 (*se piace*), 4, 8, 10, 12, 16; *Viola 2,* nos. 2, 14, 18, 20; *Viola de Brazio 2,* no. 6.

Prima Vox. Title page (fol. 1r); index (fol. 1v); music (fols. 2r–20v). *Canto,* nos. 1, 3, 5, 6, 7, 9, 12, 16 (*Canto o vero Tenore*); *Canto 1,* nos. 4, 10, 11, 17, 19; *Alto,* nos. 2, 8, 13, 14 (*Alto 1. o vero Canto*), 18; *Tenore 1,* no. 15; *Basso solo,* no. 20.

Secunda Vox. Title page (fol. 1r); index (fol. 1v); music (fols. 2r–19v). *Canto 2,* nos. 4, 10, 11, 17, 19; *Alto,* nos. 1, 3, 5, 6, 7, 9, 12, 14 (*Alto 2. o vero Tenore*); *Tenore,* nos. 2, 8, 13, 15 (*Tenore 2*).

Vox Tertia. Title page (fol. 1r); index (fol. 1v); music (fols. 2r–14r). *Alto,* no. 11; *Tenore,* nos. 1, 3, 5, 7, 9, 17; *Basso,* nos. 13 and 15; *Viola 3,* nos. 14, 18, 20.

Vox Qvarta. Title page (fol. 1r); index (fol. 1v); music (fols. 2r–8v). *Tenore,* no. 11; *Basso,* nos. 1, 3, 5, 7, 9; *Viola da gamba,* nos. 2 and 14 (*Fagotto e Viola da Gamba*); *Fagotto o vero Violone,* nos. 18 and 20.

Individual Exemplars

A. Zurich, Zentralbibliothek: AMG XIII 575. Only surviving complete copy of the 1663 edition, from the collection of the Allgemeine Musikgesellschaft Zurich. (See Georg

Walter, *Katalog der gedruckten und handschriftlichen Musikalien des 17. bis 19. Jahrhunderts im Besitze der Allgemeinen Musikgesellschaft Zürich* [Zurich: Allgemeine Musikgesellschaft, 1960].) This copy is probably identical with the one mentioned in an inventory compiled in 1697 at Berne and containing musical prints in custody of the local cantor Jonas Steiner. ("Specification jener hochobrigkeitlichen Music Bücher & Instrumenten wie solche . . . von Herrn Steiner . . . übergeben worden." Cited in Karl Nef, *Die Collegia Musica in der deutschen reformierten Schweiz von ihrer Entstehung bis zum Beginn des neunzehnten Jahrhunderts* [St. Gallen: Zollikof, 1896], 146–48.) When and in which way it came into the possession of the Allgemeine Musikgesellschaft is not documented. It should be noted, however, that a son of the above-mentioned cantor, the trumpeter, singer, and composer Johann Ludwig Steiner (ca. 1688–1761), was an active member and supporter of the Musikgesellschaft.

B. Brandenburg, Katharinenkirche (without shelf number)

One partbook (*Instrumentum Primum*) of the 1663 edition.

[C.] Sorau, Hauptkirche

One partbook (*Prima Vox*) of the 1663 edition; lost since 1916.

[D.] Inventory Ansbach 1686, fol. 1058

Secretarij Knüpffers Madrigalien. 7. Bücher. (See Richard Schaal, *Die Musikhandschriften des Ansbacher Inventars von 1686*, Quellen-Kataloge zur Musikgeschichte, 1 [Wilhelmshaven: Heinrichshoven, 1966], 79.)

[E.] Inventory Leipzig 1712

Lustige Madrigalien und Canzonetten. à 7. (See Arnold Schering, "Die alte Chorbibliothek der Thomasschule in Leipzig," *Archiv für Musikwissenschaft* 1 [1918/19]: 275–88.)

Manuscript Concordances

Inventory Ansbach 1686, fol. 1023 (see above).

   Marindgen mein leben. â 6. 3. Strom. 3 Voc. ex D x. (= no. 14)

   Ihr Sorgen weicht! â 5. 4. Str. et Basso ex F. (= no. 20)

Inventory Gotha 1691, fol. 87v (in Thüringisches Staatsarchiv Gotha, Geheimes Archiv, E XI, Nr. 65, fol. 84–93).

   Ihr Sorgen weicht ihr mörder meines lebens A[ria] Basso con 4 Violette di David Pohle (= no. 20).

Editorial Methods

The present edition is based on the copy in the Zentralbibliothek Zurich (source A). Corrections given in the errata list, published in the basso continuo, have been incorporated and reported in the critical notes. In the vocal parts the original clefs (soprano, alto, tenor) have been adapted to modern usage, while in the viola parts the treble and tenor clefs have been replaced by regular alto clefs. Short passages of the basso continuo part originally in alto or tenor clef have been tacitly transposed to bass clef. The original key signatures have been kept throughout, as they may be significant for studying the transition from the modal to the tonal system; the use of

accidentals, on the other hand, has been modernized. Editorial accidentals and articulation marks appear in brackets. Similarly, the original barlines seem to have been used quite randomly. In this edition, these have been supplied according to modern convention. A characteristic notational feature in sections in triple meter is the use of coloration to indicate hemiolas; in the transcription these are marked by open horizontal brackets.

The underlaid texts have been slightly modernized to standard German orthography and punctuation. Multiple verses in the canzonettas, which in the original print of 1663 have been set under the same music, are given as residua at the end of each piece. Single text repetitions, indicated by the *ij* symbol in the source, have been tacitly realized.

Critical Notes

Abbreviations used in this section are as follows: M(m). = measure(s), C = Canto, A = Alto, T = Tenore, B = Basso, B.c. = Basso continuo, Vn. = Violino, Va. = Viola. Pitches are given according to the system in which middle C = c′.

1. Madrigale

   M. 2, Vn. 1, note 5 is d″.   M. 6, Vn. 2, note 7 is eighth note (cf. errata).   M. 11, B.c., note 4 is A.   M. 20, Vn. 1, note 2 is half note.   M. 45, C, "sonata se piace" (all other parts have only "Sonata"); Vn. 1 and 2, no tempo indication; B.c., "allegro."   M. 53, C, A, T, B, "allegro." M. 56, B.c., note 2 is e (cf. errata).   M. 71, Vn. 1 and 2, no tempo indication.   M. 80, Vn. 1 and 2, C, A, no tempo indication.   M. 86, C, note 1 is eighth note. Mm. 90–91, Vn. 1, tempo indication in m. 91, note 5; A, tempo indication in m. 90, note 5; B.c., tempo indication in m. 90, note 1.   M. 97, Vn. 2, fermata above eighth rest.   M. 98, A, note 5 is quarter note.

2. Canzonetta

   M. 8, Va. da gamba, B.c., note 1 has ♭.   M. 40, T, whole note with half rest.

3. Madrigale

   M. 46, C, note 5 is d″.

4. Canzonetta

   M. 4, Vn. 1, beat 4 has redundant eighth note.   M. 7, B.c., note 3 is half note a (cf. errata).   M. 17, B.c., measure is repeated (cf. errata).   M. 36, C2, note 2 is f♯′.

5. Madrigale

   M. 1, A, note 1 is two quarter notes tied together. M. 3, B, note 1 is two quarter notes tied together.   M. 14, T, note 1 is two quarter notes tied together.   M. 24, T, note 1 is two quarter notes tied together.   M. 26, A, note 1 is two quarter notes tied together.   M. 33, T, note 1 is two quarter notes tied together.

6. Canzonetta

   M. 51, A, note 2 has ♯ (instead of note 3).   M. 52, A, note 2 has ♯ (instead of note 3).   M. 54, A, note 1 is g′ (cf. errata).   M. 61, A, note 1 is eighth note (cf. errata).

7. Madrigale

M. 9, C, note 1 is g♯'. M. 11, C, note 6 is eighth note (cf. errata). M. 17, C, note 3 lacks ♯ (cf. errata). M. 18, A, note is c♯. M. 25, C, note 9 is sixteenth note (cf. errata); A, notes 3, 7, and 9 are sixteenth notes (cf. errata). M. 26, B.c., note 3 is quarter note. M. 27, T, note 4 is sixteenth note (cf. errata). M. 28, T, note 3, is sixteenth note (cf. errata). M. 35, C, note 3 lacks note head (cf. errata). M. 36, T, note 3 is sixteenth note (cf. errata). M. 37, C, note 3 is sixteenth note (cf. errata). M. 38, T, note 6, is sixteenth note (cf. errata). M. 39, A, note 3, is sixteenth note (cf. errata).

8. Canzonetta

M. 1, Vn. 1, note 7 lacks ♯. M. 4, Vn. 2, note 7 lacks ♯. M. 8, T, notes 11–12 are sixteenth notes, note 13 is eighth note (cf. errata). M. 23, T, whole note with half rest. M. 27, A, T, whole notes. M. 47, A, text has "geschickt" (instead of "geschieht," cf. errata).

9. Madrigale

Mm. 1 and following, A, ♯ on middle line, for C-sharp in key signature, has been misplaced on all staves but second system (cf. errata). M. 12, B.c., note 4 has figure 9 (cf. errata). M. 49, A, note 4 is g♯'.

10. Canzonetta

M. 4, B.c., has redundant eighth note. M. 81, B.c., note 3 has figure ♭. M. 85, B.c., note 1 is quarter note. M. 99, Vn. 1, note 2 is f'.

11. Madrigale

M. 4, C1, note 1 is dotted eighth note, note 2 is sixteenth note. M. 5, A, note 2 is e'. M. 35, T, note 3 is a. M. 36, C1, C2, A, and T, lack repeat directives. M. 57, B.c., note 1 is A (cf. errata).

12. Canzonetta

M. 12, A, note 3 is g'. M. 22, B.c., note 1 is dotted whole note (cf. errata). M. 27, C, repeat directive as at final measure. M. 40, B.c., whole note. M. 41, C, A, whole note.

13. Madrigale

M. 18, B.c., note 2 is A. M. 25, A, notes 5–6, dotted eighth note and sixteenth note.

14. Canzonetta

"Alto 2. o vero Tenore" partbook is incorrectly numbered 15. M. 38, Va. 3, note 1 is g.

15. Madrigale

M. 35, T2, note 4 is quarter note with quarter rest. M. 49, T1, note 12 is eighth note. M. 58, B, note 3 is g. M. 102, B.c., note 1 has figure 6, note 2 is c.

16. Canzonetta

M. 8, B.c., note 2 has figure ♯, note 3 has figure ♮.

17. Madrigale

M. 9, C1, note 1 is eighth note, note 2 is quarter note. M. 16, T, note 1 is f. M. 20, B.c., note 4 is c. M. 32, C1, note 4 is lacking. M. 34, C2, note 6 has ♯. M. 43, B.c., note 3 has figure ♯.

18. Canzonetta

M. 1, B.c., note 1 has figure ♯ (cf. errata).

19. Madrigale

M. 1, C1, has three measures rest (cf. errata). M. 7, C2, note 2 is dotted quarter note. M. 16, C1, eighth rest is lacking. M. 70, C2, note 2 has ♯.

20. Canzonetta

M. 8, B, note 7 is eighth note. M. 14, Va. 3, whole note. M. 20, Va. 1, dotted whole note. M. 23, B.c., whole note.